AFRICAN-AMERICAN COLLECTIVE BIOGRAPHIES

Inspiring African-American Civil Rights Leaders

Stephen Feinstein

Enslow Publishers, Inc.
40 Industrial Road
Box 398
Berkeley Heights, NJ 07922
USA
http://www.enslow.com

Library of Congress Cataloging-in-Publication Data

Feinstein, Stephen.
Inspiring African-American civil rights leaders / Stephen Feinstein.
p. cm. — (African-American collective biographies)
Includes bibliographical references and index.
Summary: "Read about eight important civil rights leaders including: W. E. B. Du Bois, Philip Randolph, Martin Luther King, Jr., James Farmer, Malcolm X, John Lewis, Fannie Lou Hamer, and Thurgood Marshall"—Provided by publisher.
ISBN 978-1-59845-136-8
1. Civil rights workers—United States—Biography—Juvenile literature. 2. African Americans—Civil rights—Juvenile literature. 3. African Americans—Biography—Juvenile literature. 4. Civil rights movements—United States—History—20th century—Juvenile literature. I. Title.
E185.96.F45 2012
323.092′2—dc23
[B]

2011019952

Future editions
Paperback ISBN 978-1-4644-0035-3
ePUB ISBN 978-1-4645-0942-1
PDF ISBN 978-1-4646-0942-8

Printed in the United States of America

032012 Lake Book Manufacturing, Inc., Melrose Park, IL

10 9 8 7 6 5 4 3 2 1

To Our Readers: We have done our best to make sure all Internet Addresses in this book were active and appropriate when we went to press. However, the author and the publisher have no control over and assume no liability for the material available on those Internet sites or on other Web sites they may link to. Any comments or suggestions can be sent by e-mail to comments@enslow.com or to the address on the back cover.

Enslow Publishers, Inc., is committed to printing our books on recycled paper. The paper in every book contains 10% to 30% post-consumer waste (PCW). The cover board on the outside of each book contains 100% PCW. Our goal is to do our part to help young people and the environment too!

Photo Credits: Cover, pp. 7, 14, 19, 26, 40, 43, 48, 57, 60, 68, 78, 88, 91, 93 Library of Congress Prints and Photographs Division, Washington, D.C.; pp. 10, 21, 31, 51, 63, 71, 81 © AP Images; p. 12 Photographs in the Carol M. Highsmith Archive, Library of Congress Prints and Photographs Division; p. 29 LBJ Presidential Library, photo by Cecil Stoughton; p. 37 U.S. National Archives; p. 53 Courtesy of the Archives and Records Services Division, Mississippi Department of Archives and History; p. 73 Official White House Photo by Pete Souza; p. 83 Robert Abbott Sengstacke/Archive Photos/Getty Images.

Contents

Introduction

On January 1, 1863, during the U.S. Civil War, President Abraham Lincoln issued the Emancipation Proclamation. It declared that all slaves in those states supporting the Confederacy were now free. By May 1865, all enslaved African Americans in the United States had become free. The Civil War may have ended slavery in the United States, but African Americans' struggle for freedom and equality was just beginning.

At first, during the ten years of Reconstruction following the Civil War, black men were allowed to vote and hold public office. But when the federal government pulled its troops out of the South in 1877, white Southerners began to reestablish white supremacy. They had been angered by seeing blacks taking part in politics and holding public office. They were not ready to accept African Americans as equals.

Between 1865 and 1866, Southern states passed laws known as Black Codes to restrict the freedoms of African Americans. Blacks could not own property, could not travel freely, and could only work in certain occupations, such as farm work or domestic service. And not a single Southern state granted any African American—no matter how educated or wealthy—the right to vote.

The goal of white Southerners was to bring back the old plantation economy. While no longer slaves, most blacks now worked on the plantations as sharecroppers. Under this arrangement, black farmers were allowed to keep a portion of the crops they raised for the plantation owners. But their share was just enough to continue their labors. African Americans on the plantations lived in extreme poverty.

Jim Crow, or segregation, laws were put in place throughout the South, mandating separate facilities for blacks and whites. This meant that blacks could not use the same schools, restaurants, trains, hotels, or parks as whites. To maintain the system of segregation and white supremacy, some white Southerners turned to violence. In 1866, six former Confederate officers formed the Ku Klux Klan. Disguised in white robes and hoods, Klan members terrorized African Americans by whipping, burning, and lynching them.

African-American journalist Ida B. Wells (1862–1931), editor of a newspaper, the *Memphis Free Speech*, became a brave crusader against lynching. In 1895 she wrote "The Red Record," a pamphlet that listed the numbers of lynchings over a three-year period. Wells received death threats from angry Southern whites, and she had to flee Memphis. She settled in Chicago, where she continued to speak out against lynching. According to historian David M. Tucker, "In the long struggle against lynching, Ida B. Wells deserves more credit than any other individual for having brought this practice before the eyes of the world and, in so doing, having accelerated the establishment of law and decency in the American South."[1]

Wells and other African Americans at the time believed that progress could only come from the willingness to fight injustice. Before the American Civil War, Frederick Douglass (1818–1895), an African American who had escaped from slavery as a young man by fleeing to the North, had made an eloquent appeal for such a struggle. Speaking in Canandaigua, New York, on August 3, 1857, Douglass said,

> *The whole history of the progress of human liberty shows that all concessions yet made to her august claims, have been born of earnest struggle.…If there is no struggle there is no progress.…This struggle may be a moral one, or it may be a physical one, and*

it may be both moral and physical, but it must be a struggle. Power concedes nothing without a demand. It never did and it never will.[2]

While many African Americans were willing to struggle for their rights, others believed progress would more likely come about by not agitating or confronting the white power structure. One such individual was African-American educator Booker T. Washington (1856–1915). Born a slave, he later became the founder of the Tuskegee Institute, a school for blacks in Alabama. As the most powerful black leader in America from 1895 until his death in 1915, Washington called for a policy of accommodation. In his "Atlanta Compromise" speech in 1895, he asked for just treatment from white Southerners. In return, he offered two concessions on behalf of his fellow African Americans: Blacks should concentrate on developing work skills and not engaging in politics, and blacks should not be interested in striving for social equality.

According to Washington, "Every persecuted individual and race should get much consolation out of the great human law, which is universal and eternal, that merit, no matter under what skin found, is, in the long run, recognized and rewarded."[3] By the time of his death, Washington's ideas had been discredited among many African Americans because Southern whites had shown no inclination to compromise. It was clear that African Americans would have to struggle strenuously against discrimination and injustice.

Early in the twentieth century, many rural Southern blacks moved to cities in the South as well as the North. The National Urban League, founded in 1910, helped rural African Americans adapt to city life. The National Association for the Advancement of Colored People (NAACP), formed in 1909, waged legal battles to win voting rights for blacks. It also organized protest demonstrations. W. E. B. Du Bois, one of the founders of the NAACP, edited that organization's official magazine *The Crisis* for more than twenty years. On July 28, 1917, ten thousand African Americans marched in New York City to protest lynchings and racial discrimination.

In January 1941, A. Philip Randolph, the founder and head of the Brotherhood of Sleeping Car Porters, an all-black union, organized the March on Washington Movement (MOWM). The MOWM made plans for a huge march on Washington by African Americans to demand an end to discrimination in defense plants and segregation in the armed forces. Randolph called off the march when President Franklin Roosevelt issued Executive Order 8802, which called for an end to discrimination in government agencies, job-training

The Selma to Montgomery marches were three marches in 1965 that marked the political and emotional peak of the American civil rights movement.

programs, and by defense contractors. Segregation in the military, however, continued until July 1948, when President Harry Truman ended it with an executive order.

Although the African-American struggle for civil rights did not begin in the 1950s, the civil rights movement of the 1950s and 1960s brought about the most dramatic progress in the battle for equality and justice. On May 17, 1954, the United States Supreme Court, in *Brown* v. *Board of Education of Topeka, Kansas*, ruled that separate facilities in education were unequal. Arguing the case before the Supreme Court was Thurgood Marshall, who would become the first African-American Supreme Court justice in 1967. The Supreme Court ordered all American public schools that were segregated to be desegregated.

Although they now had federal law on their side, African-American students attempting to enter all-white schools in the South were met with bitter defiance from Southern whites. When nine African-American students tried to enter Little Rock's Central High School in 1957, Arkansas governor Orval Faubus ordered the Arkansas National Guard to block the entrance to the school. Finally, President Dwight Eisenhower had to send a thousand army troops to Little Rock to make sure the students were allowed into the school.

Meanwhile, progress toward civil rights was being made in other areas. On December 1, 1955, Rosa Parks, an African-American seamstress, was arrested in Montgomery, Alabama, when she refused to give up her seat on a bus to a white passenger. Parks was put on trial, convicted, and fined. Inspired by Parks's courageous act, Dr. Martin Luther King Jr. and other black civil rights leaders, including the Reverend Ralph D. Abernathy, organized a peaceful boycott of Montgomery's bus system. The boycott lasted until November 20, 1956, when the United States Supreme Court ruled that Alabama's bus segregation laws were unconstitutional. In 1957, Ralph

Abernathy helped King form the Southern Christian Leadership Conference (SCLC) to continue the fight against racism.

The civil rights movement of the 1950s culminated in the 1960s when the federal government enacted sweeping reforms that toppled Jim Crow, virtually eliminated public assertions of white supremacy, and boosted black pride in America. Civil rights leaders had used various strategies of nonviolent civil disobedience to challenge segregation and discrimination. The strategies included legal action, boycotts of businesses, sit-ins, and protest marches.

In 1961, the Congress of Racial Equality (CORE), led by James Farmer, organized a series of Freedom Rides. CORE's goal was to test desegregation of transportation facilities in the deep South. One of the thirteen original Freedom Riders was John Lewis, who in 1986 would be elected to the United States Congress, where he still represents Georgia's 5th Congressional District in the U.S. House of Representatives.

In 1962, the United States Supreme Court ordered that James Meredith, an African-American air force veteran, be allowed to enroll in the University of Mississippi. But the university was integrated only after President John F. Kennedy sent five thousand troops to stop the rioting that had broken out. In the summer of 1962, the Student Nonviolent Coordinating Committee (SNCC) began a program of registering black voters in Mississippi.

On August 28, 1963, Martin Luther King Jr. spoke to more than 250,000 people, black and white alike, who gathered at the Lincoln Memorial in Washington, D.C. They had participated in the March on Washington for Jobs and Freedom, organized by A. Philip Randolph, King, and other civil rights leaders. In his passionate "I Have a Dream" speech, King envisioned an America free of discrimination and injustice, a nation that in reality reflected its highest ideals. King said, "I have a dream that one day this nation will rise up and live out the true

Dr. Martin Luther King Jr. acknowledges the crowd at the Lincoln Memorial for his "I Have a Dream" speech during the March on Washington for Jobs and Freedom, Aug. 28, 1963.

meaning of its creed: 'We hold these truths to be self-evident—that all men are created equal.'"[4]

In 1964, Fannie Lou Hamer, a poor sharecropper, played a leading role in organizing Mississippi's "Freedom Summer" for SNCC. Beaten and driven from the plantation of ex-slave owners, Hamer became the vice chairman of the Mississippi Freedom Democratic Party and attended the 1964 Democratic National Convention in Atlantic City, New Jersey.

Meanwhile, Dr. King continued to lead civil rights demonstrations, including the march from Selma to Montgomery, Alabama, in March 1965. The work of King and others helped lead to the passage of such legislation as the Civil Rights Act of 1964 and the Voting Rights Act of 1965.

Unfortunately, the civil rights movement and its accomplishments provoked the fury of racist Southern whites. Many nonviolent civil rights activists became victims of violence. Among those murdered was Medgar Evers, field secretary of the NAACP.

While progress was certainly being made, many blacks in the nation's urban ghettos were becoming impatient with the pace of reform. Anger was building against racial injustices that were still commonplace. Eventually black rage exploded in numerous riots in many American cities in the North as well as the South during the summers of 1964, 1965, and 1967.

Some black leaders, including Malcolm X and Stokely Carmichael disagreed with Martin Luther King Jr.'s policy of nonviolence. They came to believe that self-defense was more important than nonviolent protest. According to Malcolm X, "when the law fails to protect Negroes from whites' attack, then those Negroes should use arms, if necessary, to defend themselves."[5]

President Barack Obama and First Lady Michelle Obama observe the 2009 Inaugural Parade. The newly elected president echoed the ideas of many civil rights–era leaders in his inaugural address.

Carmichael called for "black power." Black Panthers, members of the left-wing political organization formed by Huey Newton and Bobby Seale, became involved in shoot-outs with the police in Oakland, California.

Violence in America ultimately claimed the lives of Malcolm X, assassinated on February 21, 1965, and Martin Luther King Jr., shot and killed by a white supremacist in Memphis, Tennessee, on April 4, 1968. King's assassination led to more rioting. But eventually the nation calmed down. The civil rights movement had made undeniable progress, despite the years of turmoil.

In 1968, Shirley Chisholm became the first black woman elected to Congress. And by 1970, hundreds of African Americans had been elected to public office. In 1984 and again in 1988, Jesse Jackson, the civil rights activist who had been at Martin Luther King Jr.'s side when King was assassinated, was a candidate for the Democratic presidential nomination. Yet at the time, most Americans, blacks as well as whites, would never have imagined that on November 4, 2008, an African American—Barack Hussein Obama—would be elected president of the United States.

Speaking to a cheering crowd four days before his inauguration, Obama took note of the enormous challenges he and the nation faced and promised to act with "fierce urgency," a phrase often used by Martin Luther King Jr. Obama said that "what's required is a new declaration of independence—free from ideology and small thinking, prejudice and bigotry."[6] And in his inaugural address on January 20, 2009, President Barack Obama said, "The time has come to reaffirm our enduring spirit; to choose our better history; to carry forward that precious gift, that noble idea, passed on from generation to generation: the God-given promise that all are equal, all are free and all deserve a chance to pursue their full measure of happiness."[7]

W. E. B. Du Bois

Chapter 1

W. E. B. Du Bois

Very few African Americans lived in Great Barrington, Massachusetts, in the 1860s. At the end of the Civil War, the town's population was 3,920.[1] Perhaps that is why young William Du Bois at first was unaware that a person's color could be an issue. After all, the boys he used to play with were all white. And he and his schoolmates were the best of friends. By the time he was in high school, however, William noticed that wherever he went, somebody was bound to stare at him. The looks directed at him made him uncomfortable. William realized that people stared at him because of his color. He had brown skin, and his hair was kinky. He was different from them, a person of color.

William Edward Burghardt Du Bois was born on February 23, 1868, in Great Barrington, Massachusetts, to Alfred Du Bois and Mary Silvina Burghardt. William, who always insisted upon the "correct" pronunciation of his name, would say, "The pronunciation of my name is *Due Boyss*, with the accent on the last syllable."[2]

When William was two, his father, Alfred, left town and never returned. He wrote to Mary asking her to join him. But she had seldom been away from Great Barrington and chose to remain there. Mary was close to her extended family and did not want to leave them. William never saw his father again. Nevertheless, he had a happy childhood. He and his mother lived on his grandfather's farm outside the town. When grandfather Othello died, they moved back to town, where they lived in rooms above a stable. William called their home "upstairs."

Although William and his mother were poor, they never went hungry. When William needed schoolbooks or shoes, his uncles or aunts would pay for them. William attended school in Great Barrington from age five to age sixteen. He was one of the best students, and sometimes skipped grades. Up to this time, William had believed that the differences between people were the result of ability and hard work. After all, he had been cheered on by the town's leading citizens as he advanced in school more quickly than most of his white classmates. And he had always been welcomed into the homes of his white classmates. So when William first became aware of racial prejudice, it came as quite a shock.

Years later, in his book *The Souls of Black Folk*, Du Bois describes the incident that first made him aware of the reality of racism:

> *I remember well when the shadow swept across me.... In a wee wooden schoolhouse, something put it into the boys' and girls' heads to buy gorgeous visiting-cards—ten cents a package—and exchange. The exchange was merry, till one girl, a tall newcomer, refused my card—refused it peremptorily, with a glance. Then it dawned upon me with a certain suddenness that I was different*

from the others; or like, mayhap, in heart and life, and longing, but shut out from their world by a vast veil.[3]

When William entered high school, he got an after-school job in a local millinery shop, filling the stove with coal. He also sold newspapers after school. For a few months he served as a local correspondent for the *Springfield Republican*. Frank Hosmer, William's high-school principal, encouraged him to plan to continue his studies in college. To prepare for this, William took courses in Latin and Greek, in addition to geometry and algebra.

In the fall of 1885, William entered Fisk University, a black college in Nashville, Tennessee. His college expenses were underwritten by four Congregational churches. The student body at Fisk consisted mainly of young African-American men and women from all over the South. Students from the North, such as William Du Bois, were rare.

William had led a relatively sheltered life up in the little town of Great Barrington. Not so for his Southern classmates, however, who had been exposed to the horrors of lynching and other forms of racial hatred and hostility. Nevertheless, William was a brilliant student and was popular among his classmates. And by living in the South, he quickly learned about racial prejudice and discrimination from his own experience. William spent two summers teaching at a tiny country school for blacks in the hills of Tennessee. There he learned about the grinding poverty and drudgery of African-American rural life.

William was convinced that a good education was the only thing that could offer African Americans a better life. And he intended to get the best education possible so that someday he could serve in a leadership role for his people. So in 1888 William applied to Harvard University. He was accepted immediately and received a scholarship. At Harvard, he studied under the philosophers William James and George Santayana, and the nation's finest historians. William earned a bachelor's degree cum laude from Harvard in 1890. He then began graduate work.

From 1892 to 1894, Du Bois studied at the University of Berlin. There he met intellectuals and social scientists from all over Europe. He became interested in the socialistic ideas of Karl Marx and others. As he traveled around Europe, Du Bois experienced none of the racial prejudice that existed back at home. In 1895, he became the first African American to earn a Ph.D. from Harvard. Subsequently he began teaching at Wilberforce College in Ohio.

In 1896, Du Bois married Nina Gomer. That same year he began a study of African-American life in black neighborhoods of Philadelphia, while a non-classroom assistant in sociology at the University of Pennsylvania. In 1897 he joined the faculty of Atlanta University, where he established a department of sociology. There he taught sociology, history, economics, and political science.

In 1899 Du Bois published the results of his research in Philadelphia in his book *The Philadelphia Negro*. And in 1903, he published *The Souls of Black Folk*, a collection of his essays on the problems of being an African American in white America. Du Bois said blacks have a "double-conscious" mind in which they have to know when to act "white" and when to act "black." According to Du Bois, "One forever feels his two-ness—an American, a Negro; two souls, two thoughts, two unreconciled strivings; two warring ideals in one dark body, whose dogged strength alone keeps it from being torn asunder."[4]

Dr. W. E. B. Du Bois believed that black Americans should support the advancement of black people all over the world.

Du Bois became an outspoken critic of Booker T. Washington's policy of accommodation within the white power structure. He believed that African Americans should aspire to higher education with a focus on liberal arts, rather than Washington's recommendation of attending a trade school and acquiring job-related skills. He spoke of the black intellectuals, artists, and professionals as the "talented tenth," that 10 percent of the black population that would help achieve economic and social progress for African Americans. And instead of accepting the status quo, Du Bois felt that blacks should challenge and question whites on all grounds.

In 1905, Du Bois and William Monroe Trotter formed the Niagara Movement, dedicated to the struggle for civil rights for African Americans. The organization did not last long, because Du Bois thought whites should be included in the movement and Trotter disagreed. In 1909, Du Bois and other black leaders and white reformers formed the National Association for the Advancement of Colored People (NAACP). Based in New York City, the NAACP's main goal was to end discrimination against blacks in all areas of life in America. It worked to accomplish this through education and legal action.

In 1910 Du Bois left Atlanta University to take up full-time work for the NAACP. He traveled and lectured widely on behalf of the organization, speaking to some 96 groups totaling 35,000 people in 1911 alone. Du Bois founded *The Crisis*, the NAACP's magazine, and edited it for more than twenty years. In one of the early issues, Du Bois strongly criticized the accommodation policies of Booker T. Washington. He wrote,

> *Awful as race prejudice, lawlessness and ignorance are, we can fight them if we frankly face them and dare name them and tell the truth; but if we*

continually dodge and cloud the issue, and say the half truth because the whole stings and shames; if we do this, we invite catastrophe. Let us then in all charity but unflinching firmness set our faces against all statesmanship that looks in such directions.[5]

By 1934, as the Great Depression devastated America, his thinking had changed. He now believed that the NAACP should focus on black economic development rather than fighting discrimination. So he left the NAACP and returned to teaching at Atlanta University.

NAACP affiliates protest against a school that refused to allow students to form a campus chapter of the NAACP.

Over the years, Du Bois' views changed, and he was drawn to many different possible solutions to the problem of racism. These included integration, economic separatism, Socialism, international Communism, fighting for human rights, solidarity with third-world nations, and Pan-Africanism (the struggle against colonialism in Africa and anti-black racism in the Western hemisphere). In 1944, Du Bois returned to the NAACP, where he conducted research until 1948. Du Bois' wife Nina died in 1950, and the following year Du Bois married Shirley Graham, a distinguished writer in her own right.

In 1961, past ninety years in age, Du Bois moved to Ghana, where he began working on the creation of the *Encyclopedia Africana* for President Kwame Nkrumah. W. E. B. Du Bois died on August 27, 1963, in Accra, Ghana. It was one day before Martin Luther King Jr.'s "I Have a Dream" speech.

W. E. B. Du Bois Timeline

1868—Born on February 23, in Great Barrington, Massachusetts.

1888—Graduates from Fisk University, in Nashville, Tennessee.

1895—Becomes the first African American to receive a Ph.D. (in the subject of history) from Harvard University.

1897—Teaches sociology at Atlanta University until 1910.

1899—*The Philadelphia Negro: A Social Study* is published.

1900—Du Bois is a leader of the first Pan-African Conference in London.

1903—*The Souls of Black Folk* is published.

1905—Du Bois helps found the short-lived Niagara Movement.

1909—Helps found the NAACP. He will act as the association's director of research and editor of its magazine *The Crisis* from 1910 until 1934.

1911—Joins the Socialist party for a short period.

1934—Du Bois returns to Atlanta University to teach.

1935—Publishes *Black Reconstruction: An Essay Toward a History of the Part Which Black Folk Played in the Attempt to Reconstruct Democracy in America, 1860–1880*.

1940—Founds the magazine *Phylon* and publishes *Dusk of Dawn: An Essay Toward an Autobiography of a Race Concept*.

1944—Returns to the NAACP in a research position until 1948.

1950—Du Bois is indicted as an unregistered agent for a foreign power. He is acquitted by a federal judge the following year.

1961—Joins the Communist party, and moves to Ghana.

1963—W. E. B. Du Bois dies on August 27, in Accra, Ghana.

1968—*The Autobiography of W. E. B. Du Bois* is published.

Chapter 2

A. Philip Randolph

Ten-year-old Asa Philip Randolph and his brother, James, huddled together in the living room while their mother, Elizabeth, sat up all night with a shotgun across her lap. Their father, the Reverend James Randolph, had taken a pistol and gone with a group of men to the Duval County jail. There had been rumors that a white mob was going to break into the jail and lynch a black man who had just been locked up. At dawn Rev. Randolph returned home. He was tired but happy. He and the other African Americans had stood off the white mob and had prevented a lynching. Young Asa learned from this incident that blacks were not powerless. Indeed, this was a strong example of what could be accomplished through unity and organization, a lesson that would influence Asa's thinking in years to come.

Asa Philip Randolph was born on April 15, 1889, in Crescent City, Florida, to the Reverend James William Randolph and Elizabeth Robinson Randolph. Two years later the family moved to Jacksonville, Florida. In those days, Jacksonville was still relatively unsegregated and was considered a good place to live by African Americans. James was a minister to urban

A. Philip Randolph

handymen and rural sharecroppers, and Elizabeth was a seamstress, but the Randolphs never made much money. Although the Randolph family was poor and often in debt, they never went hungry. They produced as much of their own food as possible in the garden in the backyard, ran a meat market, and operated a dry-cleaning business.

Asa and his brother, James, who was two years older, loved to read. But their father would not allow them to read their books in the reading room of the public library. By the early 1900s, Jacksonville was rapidly becoming segregated. And among the newly segregated public facilities was the library. Randolph also insisted that his sons avoid riding on the segregated streetcars and walk instead to wherever they wanted to go in the city.

In 1903, Asa and James, aged fourteen and sixteen, entered the Cookman Institute. Cookman was the first high school for African Americans in Florida. The school taught academic subjects including Latin, Greek, French, natural sciences, philosophy, law, literature, music, and public speaking. There were also courses in survival skills such as agriculture, tailoring, shoemaking, printing, and home economics.

Asa and his brother were superior students. Asa was popular with his classmates. According to their fellow student James Parker, "The biggest crowds came out to watch baseball at Cookman when Asa Randolph was playing. I would guess he could have made a career as a baseball player, if he had wanted. With that voice of his, he could also have made a career as a singer. He was very artistic; had no interest in the trivial aspects of life."[1]

Asa and James graduated from the Cookman Institute in 1907. At the graduation, Asa was chosen class valedictorian. For the next four years, Asa worked at a variety of jobs. He worked as a clerk in a grocery store, drove a delivery wagon for a drug company, stacked logs in a lumberyard, and pushed wheelbarrows in a fertilizer factory.

Through these years of hard and often dreary work, Asa devoted his spare time to his cultural interests and keeping up with current events. He still loved to read, especially literature and history books. Asa considered W. E. B. Du Bois' *The Souls of Black Folk* to be the most influential book he ever read. He became convinced that it would be "absolutely necessary to fight for social equality."[2] This would remain a guiding principle for Randolph for the rest of his life.

Asa's other activities during this period included giving public readings of the Bible, Shakespeare, and poetry, a welcome practice in black communities with high rates of illiteracy. He delighted in singing in a barbershop quartet and acting in a dramatic group. Asa received a great deal of encouragement for his musical and acting abilities. But eventually, Asa came to believe that Jacksonville did not offer him the opportunity for the kind of life he wanted to lead. In April 1911, Asa and his friend Beaman Hearn sailed on a steamboat, the *Arapahoe*, to New York City. They washed dishes in the ship's kitchen to help pay for the voyage.

During the previous decade (1900–1910), the first large wave of black migration to northern cities had occurred. Many African Americans were eager to escape the worsening segregation and violence in the South. Because so many of the African Americans moving north were intellectuals, businessmen, and professionals, the mass movement came to be called "the migration of the Talented Tenth." By 1910, only 14,309 of Manhattan's 60,534 blacks were natives of the state of New York.[3]

President Lyndon B. Johnson presents the Medal of Freedom—the nation's highest civilian honor—to A. Philip Randolph on September 14, 1964.

Randolph and his friend Hearn found an inexpensive apartment to rent in Harlem. The two friends enjoyed the sights and sounds of the big city. Within a couple of months, however, the little money they had was gone. Hearn returned to Jacksonville. Randolph worked at a succession of low-paying jobs as a porter, an elevator operator, and a waiter. At one job on a riverboat, Randolph tried to organize the other workers to protest poor living conditions on board. As a result, he was fired.

Just as in Jacksonville, Randolph filled his spare hours with more meaningful activities. He hoped to become a professional actor. He participated in several Shakespeare productions with a theater group from the Epworth League, a youth Christian group. But Randolph soon realized that he would not become a professional actor because his parents were against the idea. And he felt he should honor their wishes.

Randolph decided to enroll at New York's City College. There he took courses in history, political science, and economics. He became interested in Socialism and the idea that wide gaps in wealth could be avoided if the government controlled the distribution of goods and services. Randolph formed his own political group, the Independent Political Council, and gave a speech about his ideas. Impressed with his speech, Ernest T. Welcome hired Randolph to work for his employment agency, the Brotherhood of Labor, which specialized in finding jobs for black newcomers.

While writing pamphlets at the Brotherhood's office, Randolph met Lucille Campbell Green, a widow who operated a successful beauty salon down the hall. In November 1914, the two married. Lucille introduced Randolph to Chandler Owen of the newly organized National Urban League, which sought to improve working conditions for African Americans. Randolph and Owen became close friends. They worked together giving speeches for the Independent Political Council. And in 1917, they started a magazine called *The Messenger*. That same year, the United States had entered World War I in Europe. Editorials in *The Messenger* were all about opposition to the war and the need for racial equality.

Randolph was a strong believer in labor unions. In the summer of 1925, *The Messenger* published two articles about the plight of African-American porters on Pullman railroad cars. At the time, Pullman was the largest employer of blacks in the nation. Black porters

A. Philip Randolph (center) speaks at a news conference for the forthcoming March on Washington with civil rights leaders Bayard Rustin (left) and Dr. John Morsell in New York City, Aug. 3, 1963.

catered to the comfort of white passengers, and relied on their tips for most of their income. On August 25, 1925, Randolph led a meeting of several hundred porters and organized a union called the Brotherhood of Sleeping Car Porters. Randolph served as president of the new union. Within two years, the union had seven thousand members. A bitter struggle between the Brotherhood and the Pullman Company lasted until 1937, when Pullman agreed to a contract with the union. Randolph's union had won significant pay increases, a shorter workweek, and overtime pay for the Pullman employees.

In 1941, to attack racism in the war to preserve international democracy, Randolph and two other civil rights leaders, Bayard Rustin and A. J. Muste, organized the March on Washington Movement (MOWM). They proposed an all-black march on Washington to protest racial discrimination in war-related industries. They also called for desegregation of the armed forces. Randolph had called for a "thundering march of 100,000 blacks on Washington to wake up and shock white America."[4] To prevent a disruptive march, on June 25, 1941, President Franklin Roosevelt ordered an end to discrimination in defense industries by issuing the Fair Employment Act. Randolph called off the march. But the military remained segregated.

At the 1948 Democratic National Convention, Randolph led a group protesting continued segregation in the military. Randolph vowed, "I am prepared to oppose a Jim Crow army till I rot in jail."[5] Soon after that, on July 26, 1948, President Harry S. Truman ordered an end to segregation in the armed forces.

In 1963, Randolph, with the help of Bayard Rustin and Martin Luther King Jr., organized the historic March on Washington for Jobs and Freedom. The march represented Randolph's two main concerns, labor issues and civil rights. King gave his dramatic "I Have a Dream" speech at the march on August 28, 1963. For the next five years, Randolph continued to be active in civil rights and union affairs until his health began to deteriorate. Randolph died on May 16, 1979.

Throughout his life, Randolph believed in the importance of struggling for freedom and justice. He said,

> *Salvation for a race, nation, or class must come from within. Freedom is never granted; it is won. Justice is never given; it is exacted. Freedom and justice must be struggled for by the oppressed of all lands and races, and the struggle must be continuous, for freedom is never a final fact, but a continuing evolving process to higher and higher levels of human, social, economic, political and religious relationships.*[6]

A. Philip Randolph Timeline

1889—Randolph is born on April 15 in Crescent City, Florida.

1891—The family moves to Jacksonville, Florida.

1911—Randolph begins to study at the City College of New York.

1914—Marries Lucille E. Green.

1917—Randolph and Chandler Owen found *The Messenger*.

1925—Randolph becomes the leader of the campaign to organize the Brotherhood of Sleeping Car Porters (BSCP). It becomes an official union in 1937.

1941—Randolph threatens to organize a March on Washington, and President Roosevelt signs Executive Order 8802 on June 25, barring discrimination in defense industries and federal bureaus.

1948—Helps convince President Harry Truman to sign Executive Order 9981 on July 26, 1948, banning segregation in the armed forces.

1957—Organizes the Prayer Pilgrimage to Washington to support civil rights efforts in the South. He also organizes the Youth March for Integrated Schools.

1963— Organizes the March on Washington, D.C., fighting for jobs and freedom. This was the site of

Martin Luther King Jr.'s famed "I Have a Dream" speech.

1979—A. Philip Randolph dies on May 16, in New York, New York.

Chapter 3

Martin Luther King Jr.

Six-year-old Martin and his best friend had played together since they were three. Among their favorite activities were flying kites, building model planes, racing their bikes, and especially playing baseball in the backyard. Although Martin's young friend didn't live in the community, his father owned a store across the street from Martin's house. And Martin's playmate was there almost every day. When the two friends turned six, they entered school. Unfortunately, the boys had to go to separate schools because they lived in segregated Atlanta. And Martin was black, and his friend was white. One day, Martin's friend told him that his father would no longer allow him to play with Martin.

The friendship was over, and Martin was in shock. Because of this and other incidents, Martin became aware of the existence of a race problem. As he grew older, he came to understand the many ways that African Americans were affected by the evils of racism. As Martin later wrote in his autobiography, "I always had

Dr. Martin Luther King Jr.

a resentment towards the system of segregation and felt that it was a grave injustice."[1]

Martin Luther King Jr. was born on January 15, 1929, in Atlanta, Georgia, to Alberta Williams King and Martin Luther King Sr. Martin's father, Reverend King, was the pastor at Ebenezer Baptist Church. His mother was a schoolteacher. Martin, his older sister, Christine, and his younger brother, Alfred Daniel, had a happy childhood. Their parents were strict but loving. From both parents, the King children learned the importance of courtesy, discipline, honesty, and hard work. The Reverend King set an example of dignity for his children, making sure they understood from an early age that they were as good as anyone else.

Much of Martin's childhood was spent in church, every Sunday and often other afternoons and evenings. There he heard his father preach. He learned how words had the power to fill people with joy or to move people to sadness or anger, to get people to think about issues of concern. Martin once told his parents, "You just wait and see. When I grow up I'm going to get me some big words."[2]

Martin also developed a love of books and reading. According to his father, "Even before he could read, he kept books around him, he just liked the idea of having them."[3] He read his father's books and borrowed books from the library. He was an outstanding student, the brightest in his class, and he skipped a few grades.

By the time Martin was in high school, he had had plenty of experience with discrimination and segregation. This included having to sit in the back of the bus, being unable to drink from "white" fountains, and being ignored or passed over in favor of white customers in a downtown store.

When Martin was fifteen, he began his freshman year at Morehouse College on September 20, 1944. At Morehouse, a school for black males in Atlanta, the emphasis was on preparation for the ministry. But at the time, Martin was not interested in becoming a minister. According to Martin, "Because of the influence of my mother and father, I guess I always had a deep urge to serve humanity, but I didn't start out with an interest to enter the ministry. I thought I could probably do it better as a lawyer or doctor."[4] But Martin's father had wanted his son to follow in his footsteps.

At Morehouse, Martin read Henry David Thoreau's essay "On Civil Disobedience." He was fascinated by the theory of nonviolent resistance and the idea of refusing to cooperate with an evil system. Through his classes with Professor George D. Kelsey, and the chapel sermons of Dr. Benjamin Mays, Martin came to believe that the church could be the most effective avenue of social protest. In his senior year, on February 25, 1948, Martin became an ordained minister at Ebenezer Baptist Church. On June 8, Martin received his bachelor of arts degree from Morehouse.

On September 14, 1948, Martin Luther King Jr. entered Crozer Theological Seminary in Chester, Pennsylvania. There he studied the social and ethical theories of all the great philosophers. He was particularly influenced by the teachings of Mahatma Gandhi, the Indian leader and social reformer, and his campaigns of nonviolent resistance in India. After graduating from Crozer on May 8, 1951, with a bachelor of divinity degree, King continued his education at Boston University's School of Theology. There he developed further his ideas of social justice for African Americans and how best to accomplish this.

In January 1952, King met Coretta Scott, an aspiring conservatory-trained soprano and Alabama native. The two fell in love and were married on June 18, 1953. The following year King became the pastor of Dexter Avenue Baptist Church in Montgomery, Alabama. There he

Dr. Martin Luther King Jr., at microphones, on the day he met with President Lyndon B. Johnson to discuss civil rights at the White House in 1963

delivered his first sermon as the Reverend Martin Luther King Jr. on May 2, 1954. On June 5, 1955, King received his doctorate in theology from Boston University. He now became Dr. Martin Luther King Jr.

King joined the local branch of the NAACP and became involved in its community program. On August 25, 1955, Rosa Parks, secretary of the Montgomery NAACP chapter, informed King of his election to the group's executive committee. Later that year, on November 17, the first of the Kings' four children, Yolanda Denise, was born.

On December 1, 1955, Parks, who in addition to her NAACP role was a seamstress who worked in a department store, was arrested for refusing to give up her seat on a bus to a white passenger. Four days later, King was elected head of a newly formed protest group, the Montgomery Improvement Association (MIA). King, Rev. Ralph Abernathy, and other black leaders in Montgomery organized a boycott of the city's bus system.

King believed that what they were preparing to do was related to the ideas of civil disobedience that Thoreau had expressed. In a speech to the MIA, King said,

> *You know, my friends, there comes a time when people get tired of being trampled over by the iron feet of oppression.... We are not afraid of what we are doing, because we are doing it within the law. There is never a time in our American democracy that we must ever think we're wrong when we protest. We reserve that right.*[5]

The bus boycott by more than 50,000 blacks lasted 381 days until December 20, 1956. In a major victory for African Americans and the civil rights movement, the United States Supreme Court then ruled that Alabama's bus segregation laws were unconstitutional. During the boycott, King's home was bombed. Fortunately nobody was hurt. King feared for the safety of his family, but decided that the struggle for civil rights was more important than anything else.

In 1957, King, Abernathy, and other black ministers formed the Southern Christian Leadership Conference (SCLC). Its purpose was to urge the federal government to pass civil rights laws and to promote the movement for black equality in the South. King was elected president of the new organization. During the next few years, as the civil rights movement grew across the South, Dr. King and the SCLC organized and led various protests.

In April 1963 in Birmingham, Alabama, King and twenty thousand other African-American civil rights activists were engaged in an anti-segregation protest. Singing "We Shall Overcome," they were attacked by the police, who used clubs, electric cattle prods, police dogs, and powerful fire hoses. Many marchers were seriously injured. About twenty-five hundred, including Dr. King, were jailed. In his "Letter from Birmingham City Jail," King wrote, "I have no fear about the outcome of our struggle in Birmingham, even if our motives are presently misunderstood. We will reach the goal of freedom in Birmingham and all over the nation, because the goal of America is freedom."[6] In the course of his career, King was arrested twenty-nine times.

Later that year, on August 28, 1963, Dr. King gave his famous "I Have a Dream" speech at the Lincoln Memorial in Washington, D.C. during the March on Washington for Jobs and Freedom. The historic march had been organized by A. Philip Randolph, King, and other civil rights leaders. Speaking to a crowd of more than 250,000, King said, "I have a dream that my four little children will one day live in a nation where they will not be judged by the color of

Dr. Martin Luther King, Jr.

their skin but by the content of their character. I have a dream today!"[7]

King continued to organize peaceful protests against racial injustice. In 1964 he won the Nobel Peace Prize. In March 1965, King led several thousand marchers from Selma to Montgomery, Alabama, in a powerful civil rights demonstration. Dr. King's work in the civil rights movement helped lead to the passage of the Civil Rights Act of 1964 and the Voting Rights Act of 1965.

Dr. King came to believe that African Americans would not be truly free until they had achieved economic as well as political equality. He spoke out against the Vietnam War, believing it was immoral and a waste of money that could be used to help eradicate poverty in America. In April 1968, he went to Memphis, Tennessee, to give his support to striking black sanitation workers. There, on April 3, he delivered a sermon at the Bishop Charles Mason Temple. King said, "I've seen the promised land. I may not get there with you. But I want you to know tonight, that we, as a people will get to the promised land."[8]

The next day, as he stood on the balcony of his motel, Dr. King was shot and killed by James Earl Ray. The man who had so strongly believed in nonviolence and peaceful protest fell victim to racist violence. In tribute to his enormous contribution to the struggle for justice and equality in America, Martin Luther King, Jr. Day of Service was established as a United States national holiday in 1983 and first celebrated in 1986. It is observed on the third Monday of January each year.

Martin Luther King, Jr. Timeline

1929—King is born in Atlanta, Georgia.

1944—Enters Morehouse College in Atlanta at the age of 15.

1948—Graduates from Morehouse College.

1951—Graduates from Crozer Theological Seminary in Chester, Pennsylvania, with a a bachelor of divinity degree.

1953—Marries Coretta Scott.

1954—Becomes a pastor for the Drexel Avenue Baptist Church in Montgomery, Alabama.

1955—The Montgomery Bus Boycott begins, and Dr. King is selected as the leader.

1957—King helps create the Southern Christian Leadership Conference.

1959—King and his wife, Coretta, are warmly received by India's Prime Minister Jawaharlal Nehru.

1960—Becomes co-pastor of the Ebenezer Baptist Church in Atlanta, Georgia. In October, he is arrested with others while protesting segregation at a lunch counter.

1963—Writes his "Letter from a Birmingham Jail" after being arrested with many others while protesting segregation at lunch counters and in hiring practices.

1963—Delivers his "I Have a Dream" speech on August 28, at the Lincoln Memorial in Washington, D.C.

1964—The Civil Rights Act of 1964 is passed. In December, King receives the Nobel Peace Prize.

1967—King commits himself irrevocably to opposing U.S. involvement in the Vietnam War.

1968—King is assassinated on April 4 in Memphis, Tennessee.

1983—Martin Luther King, Jr. Day is established on November 3. It is celebrated on the third Monday in January.

2011—The Martin Luther King, Jr. National Memorial is opened on October 16.

Chapter 4

James Farmer

James Farmer had a recurring dream. In it he trudges along an unpaved red dirt road on a hot midsummer day. He is holding onto his mother's finger as they walk. Across the street is a drugstore. James is thirsty and says, "Mommy, I want to get a Coke." His mother says to her three-year-old son, "You can't get a Coke here, Junior. Wait till we get home. There's lots of Coke in the icebox." Then James sees another little boy enter the drugstore. Through the window, he sees the boy being served a Coke at the soda fountain. He asks his mother why he can't get a Coke when the other boy could. Sadly, she tells him, "He's white. You're colored."[1] This dream, with its bitter lesson about racial **segregation** in the South, had been a reality. It would haunt James Farmer for many years to come.

James Leonard Farmer, Jr., was born on January 12, 1920, in Marshall, Texas, to James Leonard and Pearl Farmer. James's father, known as J. Leonard, was a Methodist minister and educator. He had been the first African American to earn a Ph.D. in the state of Texas.

James Farmer

He could read, write, and speak in several languages, including Hebrew, Greek, Aramaic, Latin, French, and German. When James was six months old, the family moved to Holly Springs, Mississippi, where his father got a job teaching at Rust College, a black school.

When he was four and a half, James entered the first grade. He was such an outstanding student that he was soon placed in the second grade, catching up with his sister, Helen. In 1925, the Farmers moved back to Texas. J. Leonard had gotten a job as professor of philosophy and religion at Samuel Houston College in Austin.

Two years later, James was excited by the birth of his younger brother, Nathaniel. Another event occurred that year, which was to make a lasting impression on James's mind. One Sunday after church, the Farmers drove out into the hilly country outside of Austin for a family picnic. On the way, James's father accidentally hit a pig that had suddenly run onto the road from the bushes. They didn't stop, because J. Leonard pointed out that African Americans were often killed for less.

After a while, the Farmers stopped and began their picnic on the grass near the road. Soon, a pickup truck stopped and two white men, one holding a shotgun, got out. The men demanded to be paid for the pig, their threatening speech filled with insults and contempt. When J. Leonard handed one of the men a check, he tossed it on the ground. The man demanded that J. Leonard pick it up, which he did. James, filled with anger and shame, thought to himself, "I'll never do that when I grow up. They'll have to kill me."[2]

James Farmer did so well in school that when he was fourteen he was ready for college. In 1934 he entered Wiley College in Marshall, Texas. He graduated in 1938, and having decided to study for the ministry, enrolled in Howard University in Washington, D.C. His thoughts frequently turned to the injustice of racial segregation in America. He hoped to find an effective way to fight for freedom and equality for African Americans.

While at Howard, Farmer learned how Mahatma Gandhi organized nonviolent protests to fight for India's independence from Great Britain. He became convinced that progress in America could be achieved through nonviolence and civil disobedience when laws were involved. According to Farmer, "Gandhi has the key for me to unlock the door to the American dream."[3]

In April 1941, Farmer and about thirty other national youth leaders had been invited by Eleanor Roosevelt to meet with President Franklin D. Roosevelt at the White House. After Roosevelt spoke, he invited questions from his young guests. Farmer said, "Mr. President, in your opening remarks you described Britain and France as champions of freedom. In light of their colonial policies in Africa, which give the lie to that principle, how can they be considered its defenders?" Roosevelt, not pleased by this question, replied, "In which country would *you* rather live today—France or Nazi Germany?"[4]

By his last year at Howard, Farmer had decided against a career in the ministry. In August 1941, after graduating from Howard, Farmer moved to Chicago. There he worked for the Fellowship of Reconciliation (FOR). This organization was committed to bringing about social change through nonviolence. When the United States entered World War II after the Japanese attack on Pearl Harbor, Farmer, committed to nonviolence, was a conscientious objector.

Farmer was preparing a plan for a Gandhi-type movement of nonviolent direct action against segregation and race discrimination. Farmer and several other members of FOR met in Chicago in April 1942. There they founded an organization called the Committee of Racial Equality (CORE). The new organization's black and white members elected Farmer its leader. He led several protests, including a successful one against restaurants in Chicago that refused service to blacks.

Civil rights leaders clasp hands as they sing during the closing of a memorial in New York, September 22, 1963, for four girls killed in the bombing of the Sixteenth Street Baptist Church in Birmingham, Alabama. From right: author James Baldwin; James Farmer, Congress of Racial Equality; unidentified man; and veteran Socialist leader Norman Thomas.

By 1944, CORE had established chapters in cities across the country. The organization had grown larger and it changed its name to the Congress of Racial Equality. Later that year, however, Farmer resigned as CORE's national director because others in the group opposed his ideas for massive protests.

In 1949, Farmer married Lula Peterson. For the next several years Farmer worked as an organizer for labor unions. During the 1950s Farmer served as national secretary of the Student League for Industrial Democracy (SLID). Then in 1959, he became program director at the National Association for the Advancement of Colored People (NAACP).

Meanwhile in 1947, CORE had organized the Journey of Reconciliation. CORE sent eight black and eight white men on an unsuccessful bus trip through the upper South to challenge segregation in transportation. In December 1960, the United States Supreme Court outlawed racial segregation in train stations and bus terminals. But the South continued its policies of segregation regardless of the law. On February 1, 1961, Farmer was reelected as the national director of CORE. That year he organized a series of Freedom Rides. This time, the thirteen volunteer Freedom Riders, men and women, would ride buses through the deep South. Seven Freedom Riders were black, six were white.

In Anniston, Alabama, one of the two Freedom Ride buses was set on fire. The Freedom Riders were severely beaten by angry white mobs in Anniston, as well as in Birmingham and Montgomery. One thousand members of the National Guard, sent by the federal government, escorted the Freedom Riders on the last leg of the journey to the Mississippi line.

In Mississippi, Farmer and the Freedom Riders spent six weeks in jail. But the Freedom Riders had accomplished their goal. By the end of the summer of 1961, more than a thousand people had taken part in Freedom Rides. Attorney General Robert Kennedy ordered federal agencies to begin enforcing the Supreme Court ruling banning segregated bus and train stations. By the end of the following year, bus and train stations throughout the South were no longer segregated.

The Freedom Rides had received national and international attention, and Farmer became a well-known civil rights leader. He pushed for greater job opportunities for African Americans in the North and in the South.

Booking photos of James Farmer from his May 24, 1961, arrest while participating in the Freedom Rides

In 1963 Farmer was one of the organizers of the huge March on Washington for Jobs and Freedom. In 1966, he resigned as director of CORE after it began falling apart due to unsolvable problems relating to internal organization, disagreements over member reactions to real life-threatening violence in the Deep South, and American military involvement in Vietnam.

In 1969 President Richard M. Nixon appointed Farmer as assistant secretary of the Department of Health, Education, and Welfare. He resigned in 1971 and supported himself through lectures and writing. In 1984, Farmer became a history professor at Mary Washington College (now the University of Mary Washington) in Fredericksburg, Virginia. He taught there until 1998. That year, President Bill Clinton awarded him the Presidential Medal of Freedom. On July 9, 1999, James Farmer died of complications from diabetes.

Farmer, in a concise statement in his autobiography, pointed to his accomplishments: "From the early days in Holly Springs to the ebbtide years of the present, like all who have fought to cleanse this nation, I have helped to pave the roads on which America's black children walk toward new vistas that I shared in shaping."[5]

James Farmer Timeline

1920—Farmer is born on January 12 in Marshall, Texas.

1938—Earns a Bachelor of Science (BS) degree from Wiley College.

1941—Receives the Bachelor of Divinity (BD) degree from Howard University School of Religion.

1942—Establishes the Committee (later Congress) of Racial Equality (CORE).

1949—Marries Lula A. Peterson.

1961—Serves as National Director of CORE until 1966. He participates in Freedom Rides throughout the South.

1965—*Freedom When* is published.

1968—Farmer runs for Congress, but does not win.

1984—Teaches at Mary Washington College until 1998.

1985—*Lay Bare the Heart: An Autobiography of the Civil Rights Movement* is published.

1998—Farmer receives the Presidential Medal of Freedom.

1999—James Farmer dies at Mary Washington Hospital in Fredericksburg, Virginia, on July 9.

Chapter 5

Malcolm X

One day, Malcolm's seventh-grade English teacher, Mr. Ostrowski, asked him if he had given any thought to a career. Malcolm was one of the smartest students in the class. He told his teacher he was thinking of becoming a lawyer. Mr. Ostrowski looked surprised. He said,

> *Malcolm, one of life's first needs is for us to be realistic.... A lawyer—that's no realistic goal for a nigger. You need to think about something you can be. You're good with your hands—making things. Everybody admires your carpentry shop work. Why don't you plan on carpentry? People like you as a person—you'd get all kinds of work.*[1]

Malcolm was stunned. He had believed that Mr. Ostrowski liked him. Now Malcolm suddenly understood that even well-meaning white people held racist notions regarding African Americans. In the eyes of whites, he would always be a second-class citizen. It was a bitter lesson, one that Malcolm would never forget.

Malcolm Little was born on May 19, 1925, to Earl and Louise Little in Omaha, Nebraska. Malcolm was the

Malcolm X

fourth of the Littles' seven children (Earl, an itinerant minster and construction worker, also had three other children from a previous marriage, who lived in Boston). Shortly after Malcolm was born, the family moved to Milwaukee. They stayed there briefly and then moved on to Lansing, Michigan.

Louise later told Malcolm about a frightful event that occurred in Omaha when she was pregnant with him. One night, a group of hooded Ku Klux Klan riders on horseback armed with shotguns and rifles surrounded the house. They demanded to speak to Earl. Apparently they were angry that Earl, a Baptist preacher, had been spreading the ideas of Marcus Garvey. Garvey had been speaking out about how African Americans could improve their lives, and he was urging African Americans to move to Africa. When a terrified Louise told them Earl was not home, the Klansmen warned the Littles that they had better get out of town. Then the Klansmen rode off into the night, but not until they had shattered every windowpane in the house.

On November 7, 1929, the Littles' home in Lansing was set on fire during the night. Earl Little fired shots at the two white men who had set the fire and were running away. When the white police and firemen arrived, they just stood around and watched as the house burned to the ground. The Little family next moved to East Lansing, where Earl, with his own hands, built a four-room house in the country about two miles outside of town. This was the home in which Malcolm grew up.

One day in September 1931, tragedy struck. Earl Little was killed in an accident, crushed to death by a trolley. There were rumors that Earl had been killed first and his body placed on the trolley tracks. He had made enemies by speaking up for the rights of African Americans. Life now became difficult for Louise Little and her children. The country was in the midst of the Great Depression, and there were many days when the Littles went hungry. By 1937 it became clear that Louise was drifting toward insanity and could no longer support the family. Social workers sent the children to live in different foster homes. Louise Little spent twenty-six years in a mental hospital in Kalamazoo, Michigan.

In 1941, when he was sixteen, Malcolm went to Boston to live with his half-sister Ella. She lived in a black section of the city known as Roxbury. Malcolm had never lived in a big city before, and he was excited by city life. According to Malcolm, "I spent the first month in town with my mouth hanging open. The sharp-dressed young 'cats' who hung on the corners and in the poolrooms, bars and restaurants, and who obviously didn't work anywhere, completely entranced me."[2]

Malcolm met a young African American called Shorty, and the two became friends. They hung out in pool halls and on the streets. Malcolm picked up a lot of street talk from Shorty and his friends, and he began using it. For the first time in his life, Malcolm drank liquor, smoked cigarettes and reefers (marijuana cigarettes), and played cards. Because image was important in this world, Malcolm wanted to look cool like the other young black men he met. So he had his red hair straightened and bought a blue zoot suit.

Shorty showed Malcolm how to survive on the streets, how to hustle up a dollar. He also got Malcolm a job as a shoeshine boy at the Roseland State Ballroom. There Malcolm got to listen to some of the most famous bands of the time, including Duke Ellington's and Count Basie's. Malcolm did other odd jobs, including working as a busboy and as a soda jerk in a drugstore.

Malcolm then got a job selling sandwiches on the Yankee Clipper railroad service running between Boston and New York City. Malcolm had always wanted to see New York. Once there, he took a cab up to Harlem, where he saw the show at the famous Apollo Theater. He was thrilled by the sights and sounds of the Big Apple,

Malcolm X and Martin Luther King, Jr., waiting for a press conference in 1964

especially Harlem. Malcolm wrote, "But New York was heaven to me. And Harlem was Seventh Heaven!"[3]

In 1943 Malcolm moved to New York. He got a job as a waiter at Small's Paradise, a popular Harlem nightclub. Malcolm became known as "Detroit Red." Unfortunately, he became involved in criminal activity, selling drugs and pulling robberies and stickups. In 1945 Malcolm returned to Boston, after running into trouble with New York gangs.

Back in Boston, Malcolm, Shorty, and some other friends burglarized homes. Eventually, on January 12, 1946, Malcolm was arrested when he was caught with stolen jewelry, fur coats, and other items. He was also charged with illegal possession of guns. At his trial in February 1946, Malcolm received a sentence of eight to ten years.

Malcolm began serving his sentence at the Charlestown State Prison. He used his time to read as much as he could. Prison authorities eventually allowed Malcolm to be transferred to a prison in Norfolk that had begun an experimental prison reform program. The Norfolk Prison Colony had an excellent library. Malcolm now had the opportunity to read and to think. He used a dictionary to teach himself any unfamiliar words. Malcolm read the writings of the world's greatest philosophers. He read biographies of the great leaders throughout history. And he read about the world's great religions, including Islam.

Malcolm's brother Reginald visited him in prison. Reginald had become a minister in the Nation of Islam. The religious sect known as the Nation of Islam (NOI) was created in 1930 in Detroit by W. D. Fard, also known as Master Farad Muhammad. Fard appointed Elijah Poole, renamed Elijah Muhammad, to succeed him as leader of the group. The Nation of Islam differed from mainstream

Islam (Sunni or Shia) through its racist teachings that reduced the white man to the status of devil. Indeed, Reginald told Malcolm, "The white man is the devil."[4]

Every day, Malcolm received letters from his brothers and sisters. Like Reginald, they had all converted to the NOI. They urged Malcolm to accept the teachings of Elijah Muhammad, who had already begun recruiting prisoners for the NOI. Malcolm wrote a letter to Elijah Muhammad and they began a correspondence. Malcolm's conversion to the NOI in 1948 gave him a new purpose in life. Once out of prison, he would recruit new members to the NOI.

When Malcolm was released from prison on parole on August 7, 1952, he moved to Detroit. There, he lived with his brother Wilfred, who got him a job selling furniture. The following year, Malcolm began attending NOI meetings and working to increase the membership of the local NOI temple.

At this time, Malcolm changed his name from Malcolm Little to Malcolm X. According to Malcolm, "The Muslim's 'X' symbolized the true African family name that he never could know. For me, my 'X' replaced the white slavemaster name of 'Little'....The receipt of my 'X' meant that forever after in the nation of Islam, I would be known as Malcolm X."[5]

Because Malcolm was a passionate and persuasive speaker, he was very successful in recruiting new members to the NOI. In 1953 Malcolm moved to Chicago, where he lived with Elijah Muhammad. In September of that year he became minister of the NOI temple in Boston.

In 1954, Muhammad sent Malcolm to Harlem to build up the local NOI mosque. There Malcolm met Sister Betty Shabazz (formerly Sanders). The two were married in Lansing on January 14, 1958. They would have four daughters. Malcolm became the most dynamic

Malcolm X at a news conference at the Islamic Cultural Centre after arriving in London, England, July 10, 1964

and successful minister in the NOI. He organized temples, raised funds, recruited new members, and acted as Muhammad's principal spokesman and representative.

Malcolm's message put a strong emphasis on racial pride, self-discipline, and political and economic self-determination. He preached separation of the races, and that integration was not the way to achieve freedom. Rather, revolution, not nonviolent protest, was called for, and blacks must defend themselves with arms if necessary.

By 1963, Malcolm and Elijah Muhammad began moving apart. Malcolm had learned of Muhammad's extramarital affairs and that he had fathered children with three of his former secretaries. Muhammad disapproved of some of the political ideas in Malcolm's speeches, and he began to see the younger leader as a threat to his own power in the NOI. In March 1964, Malcolm left the NOI and formed the Muslim Mosque, Inc.

In April 1964, Malcolm went on a pilgrimage to Mecca, Saudi Arabia. He also traveled to many African nations, where he was treated as if he were a head of state. On the trip, he used the name El-Hajj Malik El-Shabazz. While in Mecca, he changed his opinion about white people and his view of separatism. He realized that Muslims were of all colors and that black and white Muslims could coexist in brotherhood.

Back in America, on June 28, 1964, Malcolm formed the Organization of Afro-American Unity (OAAU) to help in the civil rights struggle. He demanded that the United Nations Commission on Human Rights launch an investigation into racial affairs in the United States. According to writer Adam Fairclough, "He renounced the idea that all whites were 'devils,' embraced orthodox Islam, and modified his views on violence. . . . He edged toward a rapprochement with the Civil Rights Movement; shortly before his death he visited Selma while King was in jail there."[6]

Malcolm often said that his radical militancy made Martin Luther King Jr.'s demands seem more reasonable to those in power. Malcolm presented himself as a model of what a self-respecting African-American male should be, unflinching in his opposition to racism and uwavering in struggle to end it.

On February 14, 1965, Malcolm's home was firebombed, but nobody was hurt. Malcolm knew that he could be killed at any time. Working on his autobiography at the time, he wrote, "Every morning when I wake up, now, I regard it as having another borrowed day. In any city, wherever I go, making speeches, holding meetings of my organization, or attending to other business, black men are watching every move I make, awaiting their chance to kill me."[7]

On February 21, 1965, three gunmen shot Malcolm to death as he was about to give a speech at the Manhattan Audubon Ballroom. The gunmen, who were arrested and convicted, were members of the NOI.

On January 20, 1999, the U.S. Postal Service issued a special commemorative stamp honoring Malcolm X. S. David Fineman, member of the Board of Governors of the U.S. Postal Service, said that Malcolm X

> *was a passionate and persuasive voice for change, and his controversial ideas helped bring race relations to a national stage. Malcolm X poured his energy and anger into speaking the truth about the plight of African Americans.... We must never forget the challenge Malcolm X issued to us. "Let us learn to live together in justice and love."*[8]

Malcolm X Timeline

1925—Malcolm Little is born on May 19, in Omaha, Nebraska.

1939— Malcolm's mother, Louise Little, is committed to an insane asylum. Malcolm and his siblings are sent to live with relatives.

1941—Malcolm moves to Boston to live with his sister.

1943—Malcolm moves to New York City, and becomes involved in various criminal activites.

1945—Little moves back to Boston after getting in trouble with some gangs in New York.

1946—Little gets arrested in Boston and goes to prison. While there, he converts to the Nation of Islam.

1952—Little is released from prison and changes his name to Malcolm X. He begins organizing temples for the Nation of Islam in various cities.

1958—Malcolm X marries Betty Shabazz.

1963—Malcolm X discovers that his mentor, and the leader of the Nation of Islam, Elijah Muhammad, was having affairs with women who worked for the Nation of Islam.

1964—Malcolm X leaves the Nation of Islam and founds the Muslim Mosque, Inc.

1964—Malcolm X goes on a pilgrimage to Mecca, Saudi Arabia. He embraces Sunni Islam, adopting the Muslim name El-Hajj Malik El-Shabazz.

1964—Malcolm X founds the Organization of Afro-American Unity.

1965—Malcolm X is assassinated on February 21, in New York, New York. *The Autobiography of Malcolm X* is published.

1992—The movie, *Malcolm X*, with Denzel Washington, is released.

John Lewis

Chapter 6

John Lewis

John Lewis spent much of his childhood picking cotton with his family. According to his vivid description,

> *You had to bend down to pick cotton. Eight to ten hours of stooping like that and your back would be on fire. It would ache all night, and it would still be aching when you got up the next morning to go out and do it all over again. There were some who beat the bending by wrapping makeshift padding around their knees and crawling up and down those rows all day long. But they then had to deal with a different kind of pain—a sharp stabbing in their legs and knees. And we all came home each night with fingertips chewed ragged and bloody by the sharp edges of those cotton pods.*[1]

John Lewis was not happy about sharecropping work. Young John felt that nobody should have to work like this. He later wrote,

> *Even a six-year-old could tell that this sharecropper's life was nothing but a bottomless pit. I watched my father sink deeper and deeper into debt, and it broke my heart. More than that, it made me angry. There was no way to get ahead with this kind of farming. The best*

> *you could do was do it well enough to keep doing it. That looked like no kind of life to me, and I didn't keep my opinion to myself. Early on, to the dismay of the rest of my family, I would speak out against what we were doing right there in the fields.*[2]

John Lewis was born on February 21, 1940, in rural Pike County, Alabama, to Eddie and Willie Mae Lewis. He was the third of ten children. The Lewis family lived in an area called Carter's Quarters. All of the neighbors belonged to the Lewis's extended family. Until John was six, the only two white people he saw were the mailman and a traveling merchant. Until he was old enough to work in the fields, John had a happy childhood.

In 1956, when John was sixteen, he was shocked by the murder of Dr. Thomas Brewer, a distant relative who lived in Columbus, Georgia. Dr. Brewer was killed by a member of the Ku Klux Klan because of his leadership role in the local branch of the NAACP. The man who admitted the shooting was never indicted. John was horrified and angered by the realization that such hatred could exist. The incident spurred him to action. He wrote a petition stating that the Pike County Public Library should be opened to blacks. Then he mailed away an application for youth membership in the NAACP.

That same year John became an ordained Baptist minister. As he later explained,

> *I had come to resent segregation and discrimination at an early age. We had the poor schools, the run-down school buses, the unpaved roads; and I saw that those were penalties imposed on us because of race. So race was closely tied to my decision to be a minister. I thought religion could be something meaningful, and I wanted to use the emotional energy of the black church to end segregation and gain freedom for black people.*[3]

Six leaders of the nation's largest black civil rights organizations meet in New York's Hotel Roosevelt on July 2, 1963, to plan a civil rights march on Washington. From left, are: John Lewis, Whitney Young, A. Philip Randolph, Dr. Martin Luther King Jr., James Farmer, and Roy Wilkins.

In September 1957, Lewis entered the American Baptist Theological Seminary (ABT) in Nashville, Tennessee. There he studied religion and philosophy. The teachings of Mahatma Gandhi regarding nonviolence and passive resistance made a deep impression on him. At the time, the person he most admired was Martin Luther King Jr., who represented everything Lewis wanted to be. Like King, Lewis felt that "we need to be less concerned with getting people up to those streets paved with gold and more concerned about what people are dealing with right down here on the streets of Nashville."[4]

In 1959 Lewis participated in a workshop on nonviolence given by James Lawson, then a teacher at Vanderbilt Divinity School. The following year, Lewis helped organize the Nashville student movement, which staged some of the first sit-ins at segregated lunch counters in Nashville and other cities. On April 15–17, 1960, the Student Nonviolent Coordinating Committee (SNCC) was formed by students meeting at Shaw University in Raleigh, North Carolina. Lewis was present at the meeting. The organization's goal was to oppose racial segregation through nonviolence.

In 1961, the Congress of Racial Equality (CORE) organized a series of Freedom Rides. The goal of the Freedom Rides was to ride buses through the deep South, challenging segregated facilities. On the first Freedom Ride, one of the thirteen volunteer Freedom Riders was John Lewis. In Rock Hill, South Carolina, Lewis was attacked by white hoodlums when he entered the white waiting room. At the bus station in Montgomery, Alabama, Lewis was knocked to the ground unconscious when a white mob attacked the Freedom Riders. He suffered a gash in the back of his head.

Then in Mississippi, Lewis and the other Freedom Riders spent six weeks in jail. But the Freedom Riders, through their tactic of nonviolence, had by the end of the year accomplished their goal. The federal government began enforcing the Supreme Court ruling banning segregated bus and train stations.

In 1962, SNCC began a program of registering black voters in Mississippi. The following year, members of

President Barack Obama signs the Civil Rights History Project Act of 2009 into law on May 12, 2009. With President Obama are, from left: Rep. Mike Quigley, Rep. Carolyn McCarthy, Rep. Sanford Bishop, Rep. Lacy Clay, Rep. Jim Clyburn, and Rep. John Lewis.

SNCC elected Lewis as their chairman. The Freedom Riders set up "freedom schools" in black communities to provide information about voters' rights. On August 28, 1963, Lewis gave a rousing speech in Washington, D.C., during the huge March on Washington for Jobs and Freedom.

In his speech, Lewis said,

> *The revolution is at hand, and we must free ourselves of the chains of political and economic slavery. The non-violent revolution is saying, "We will not wait for the courts to act, for we have been waiting for hundreds of years. We will not wait for the President, the Justice Department, nor Congress, but we will take matters into our own hands and create a source of power, outside of any national structure, that could and would assure us a victory."*[5]

On March 7, 1965, Lewis and members of SNCC marched with Dr. Martin Luther King Jr., and several hundred Freedom Riders from Selma to Montgomery, Alabama. The marchers were brutally attacked by Alabama state troopers. On the day that became known as "Bloody Sunday," many were badly injured, including Lewis, whose skull was fractured. Most Americans viewing this event on TV news were disgusted by the violence directed at peaceful protestors. The federal government felt pressured to pass the Voting Rights Act of 1965.

In 1966, Stokely Carmichael became the chairman of the SNCC. Carmichael called for "black power" and urged African Americans to arm themselves for self-defense. It now became clear that the SNCC had abandoned its devotion to nonviolence. Lewis, remaining true to his beliefs, left the organization, which faced contradictory demands from regional chapters North and South. He spent the next few years in various community organizing efforts and voter education projects. Opposing the Vietnam War, Lewis spoke out against it. On December 21, 1968, he married Lillian Miles.

From 1978 till 1980, Lewis had a job in President Jimmy Carter's administration. He worked as associate director of ACTION, responsible for running the VISTA program, the Retired Senior Volunteer Program, and the Foster Grandparent Program. In 1981 he was elected to the Atlanta city council. In 1986 Lewis was elected to Congress, defeating Julian Bond, who had also been a member of SNCC. Lewis became a member of the U.S. House of Representatives, where he continues to represent Georgia's 5th Congressional District.

As Lewis looked back at the progress he and others helped to accomplish through their courageous acts of nonviolent protest, he pointed out that

> *The government can respond. We proved it with the civil rights movement. The changes we brought about have been enormous. No one, but no one, who was born in America forty or fifty or sixty years ago and who grew up and came through what I came through, who witnessed the changes I witnessed, can possibly say that America is not a far better place than it was. We live in a different country than the one I grew up in.*[6]

John Lewis Timeline

1940—Lewis is born on February 21, outside of Troy, Alabama.

1957—Attends American Baptist Theological Seminary (ABT) in Nashville, Tennessee.

1960—Helps organize the Nashville student movement, which staged some of the first sit-ins at segregated lunch counters in Nashville and other cities.

1961—Joins the first Freedom Ride through the South. He is attacked, knocked unconscious, and arrested during the ride.

1963—Lewis is elected chairman of the Student Nonviolent Coordinating Committee (SNCC). He is dubbed one of the Big Six leaders of the civil rights movement. (The others were Whitney Young, A. Philip Randolph, Martin Luther King Jr., James Farmer, and Roy Wilkins.)

1964—Coordinates SNCC efforts to organize voter registration drives and community action programs during the Mississippi Freedom Summer.

1965— Lewis and members of the SNCC march with Dr. Martin Luther King Jr., and several hundred

Freedom Riders from Selma to Montgomery, Alabama.

1966—Lewis leaves the SNCC due to differences of opinion.

1968—Marries Lillian Miles.

1978—Works in the administration of President Jimmy Carter. As associate director of ACTION, he is responsible for running the VISTA program, the Retired Senior Volunteer Program, and the Foster Grandparent Program.

1981— Lewis is elected to the Atlanta city council.

1986—Lewis is elected to Congress as U.S. Representative of Georgia's Fifth Congressional District.

1998—Lewis's biography, *Walking With The Wind: A Memoir of the Movement*, is published.

2011—Lewis receives the Presidential Medal of Freedom.

Fannie Lou Hamer

Chapter 7

Fannie Lou Hamer

Fannie Lou Hamer described how she first started working in the cotton fields when she was a little girl.

> *I never will forget, one day—I was six years old and I was playing beside the road and this plantation owner drove up to me and stopped and asked me, could I pick cotton? I told him I didn't know and he said, "Yes, you can. I will give you things that you want from the commissary store," and he named things like Crackerjacks and sardines. So I picked the 30 pounds of cotton that week, but I found out what actually happened was he was trapping me into beginning the work I was to keep doing, and I never did get out of his debt again. By the time I was 13, I was picking two and three hundred pounds.*[1]

Fannie Lou Hamer was born on October 6, 1917, in Montgomery County, Mississippi, to Jim and Ella Townsend. She was the youngest of the Townsends' twenty children. When Fannie Lou was two, the family moved to Sunflower County. She lived there for the rest of her life. The Townsends were sharecroppers. The whole family did backbreaking work in the fields. People who worked the land had to "share" the crops, giving half of what they grew to the landowner. Sharecropping was a difficult life, but it provided the only work available for many African Americans living in the rural South.

The Townsend family picked huge amounts of cotton. One year they managed to make some money. Jim rented some land where the family could keep more of the crop for themselves. They moved into the house on the land. Jim bought three mules, a cow, a wagon, some plow tools, and a car. The family had never done this well before. But one night, while they were away from home, somebody poisoned their animals. According to Fannie Lou, "That poisoning knocked us right back down flat. We never did get back up again. That white man did it just because we were getting somewhere. White people never like to see Negroes get a little success."[2]

Fannie Lou learned to read and write in school. But when she was thirteen, she left school to work full-time with her family in the fields. After her father died in 1939, life became even more difficult for the Townsends. One day while working in the field, Fannie Lou's mother suffered an injury to her eye that would eventually cause her to lose her sight. Fannie Lou now resented the sharecropping system more than ever. She recalled,

> *I began to get sicker and sicker of the system there. I used to see my mother wear clothes that would have so many patches on them, they had been done over and over and over again. She would do that but she would try to keep us decent. She would be ragged and I always said if I lived to get grown and had a chance, I was going to try to get something for my mother and I was going to do something for the black man of the South if it would cost my life; I was determined to see that things were changed.*[3]

Fannie Lou Hamer speaks to Mississippi Freedom Democratic Party sympathizers outside the Capitol in Washington, September 17, 1965, after the House of Representatives rejected a challenge to the 1964 election of five Mississippi representatives. Hamer and two other African-American women were seated on the floor of the House while the challenge was being considered. She said, "We'll come back year after year until we are allowed our rights as citizens."[4] The challengers claimed that African Americans were excluded from the election process in Mississippi.

In 1944, at age twenty-seven, Fannie Lou married Perry "Pap" Hamer. The two settled on the W. D. Marlow plantation outside Ruleville, Mississippi. For the next eighteen years, Fannie Lou Hamer and her husband worked in the cotton fields. She was also the plantation's timekeeper, keeping records of hours worked, number of bales picked by each worker, and the pay due to each. During the 1950s, the Hamers adopted and raised daughters Dorothy Jean and Vergie.

In mid-August 1962, Charles McLaurin from the Student Nonviolent Coordinating Committee (SNCC) arrived in Ruleville. He held a meeting in which he urged people to register to vote. Hamer was at the meeting and decided to do it. She and seventeen others went to Indianola, Mississippi, to register on August 31. The trip was organized by SNCC worker Robert Moses. In Indianola, they all failed the literacy test, which was required at the time. When Hamer returned home, Marlow, the plantation owner, ordered her to either withdraw her voter application or leave the plantation. She chose to leave.

Soon Perry Hamer was also ordered off the plantation. Friends found a home for the Hamers in Ruleville. They had a roof over their heads, but they had no jobs and no money. Fannie Lou Hamer became a field secretary for SNCC. She organized a local poverty program and in the fields and churches she told people about their right to vote. In December Hamer failed a voter registration test again. But on January 10, 1963, after studying the Mississippi state constitution, she passed the test. However, on Election Day that fall, she still was unable to vote because she didn't have the money to pay the Mississippi poll tax.

In June 1963 Hamer and other SNCC workers went to Charleston, South Carolina, for a voter registration workshop. On the way back, she and the others were arrested at the bus station in Winona, Mississippi. In the police station, they were brutally beaten, and Hamer sustained serious injuries from which she would never fully recover. She was released after being held in jail for

Joining the protest outside of Convention Hall over seating of Mississippi delegates are, left to right, Fannie Lou Hamer of Mississippi and the parents of slain civil rights worker Michael Schwerner. Hamer spoke for the Mississippi Freedom Democratic Party, which had been denied seats at the Convention.

three days. As soon as she was physically well enough, Hamer continued her work for SNCC.

In 1964, SNCC organized "Freedom Summer" in Mississippi. Northern white students were recruited to set up "Freedom Schools" to educate African Americans about their rights and to organize voter-registration drives. That year, SNCC organized the Mississippi Freedom Democratic Party (MFDP) to challenge the all-white regular Mississippi Democratic Party at the Democratic National Convention in Atlantic City, New Jersey.

As vice chairman of the MFDP, Hamer testified at the convention's credentials committee hearing on August 22. She spoke of how she attempted to register to vote, lost her job, and later was jailed and beaten. She said,

> *All of this is on account we want to register, to become first-class citizens....If the Freedom Democratic Party is not seated now, I question America. Is this America? The land of the free and the home of the brave? Where we have to sleep with our telephone off the hook because our lives be threatened daily because we want to live as decent human beings, in America?*[5]

Hamer was bitterly disappointed when the convention turned down the MFDP's bid to replace the all-white Democratic Party as the legitimate Democratic representatives of the state of Mississippi. However, the convention proposed to seat two of the MFDP leaders as delegates at large, to require the Mississippi regulars to sign an oath of loyalty to the party ticket, and to revise the party's rules to eliminate racial discrimination in the selection of delegates. The white Mississippians refused to sign the loyalty oath and walked out of the convention. Thanks to the hard work of Hamer and the MFDP, the 1968 Democratic National Convention barred the white regulars, and seated the civil rights-based challengers.

In the fall of 1964, Hamer joined a SNCC delegation on a tour of Guinea and other African nations governed by blacks. She was impressed to see blacks doing jobs that she had only seen whites doing in America. She returned to the United States, determined to continue various activities involved in community organizing.

Hamer was politically active for the rest of her life. In 1965 she led a challenge to the seating of five white Mississippi congressmen by the U.S. House of Representatives. The challenge failed, but she continued to push for reforms. On August 20, 1968, Hamer was seated as a delegate at the Democratic National Convention in Chicago, where she spoke on behalf of a challenge to the Alabama delegation. In the fall of 1971 she ran unsuccessfully for Mississippi state senate. In July 1972 she was a delegate to the Democratic National Convention in Miami Beach.

Fannie Lou Hamer died on March 14, 1977, of heart failure brought on by cancer, diabetes, and hypertension.

John Lewis spoke of Fannie Lou Hamer's love of her country. He said, "She had this knowledge of the Constitution, what this country was supposed to be. She would talk about it. 'Live up to the creed. Live up to the Declaration of Independence, to the Bill of Rights.' I think she really believed in America and wanted to make it real."[6]

Fannie Lou Hamer Timeline

1917—Hamer is born on October 6, in Montgomery County, Mississippi.

1944—Hamer marries Perry "Pap" Hamer.

1962—Hamer attends a protest meeting.

1963—Hamer and others are arrested and beaten after leaving a voter registration workshop in Charleston, South Carolina, in June.

1964—Hamer helps found the Mississippi Freedom Democratic Party.

1964, 1965—Hamer runs for Congress in Mississippi, but is unsuccessful.

1968—Hamer is the Democratic National Committee representative until 1971.

1971—Hamer runs for Mississippi state senate.

1972—Hamer is a delegate to the Democratic National Convention.

1977—Hamer dies of heart failure brought on by cancer and diabetes on March 14 in Mound Bayou, Mississippi.

Chapter 8

Thurgood Marshall

Thurgood Marshall was a good student in high school. But he liked to fool around, often teasing the other kids. This behavior sometimes got him into trouble. Once, the principal punished Thurgood by sending him down into the basement. He handed Thurgood a copy of the U.S. Constitution and told him he could not come up out of the basement until he had memorized it. Marshall later said, "Before I left that school, I knew the whole thing by heart."[1]

According to writer Juan Williams, "Thurgood's study of the Constitution gave him an interesting perspective on the conflict between American ideals and the reality of how the law was twisted when it came to black people."[2] From his second-floor classroom window, Thurgood often watched the goings-on at the police station next door. It was clear that most of the prisoners brought in by the all-white police were black. Often he could hear the police beating up the prisoners.

Thurgood's father, Willie, a dining-car waiter on the railroad, then a Baltimore-based waiter at a fancy

Thurgood Marshall in 1957

whites-only club, was very interested in the courts. He spent much of his spare time seated in the courtroom, watching trials. At home, he would engage his two sons in debates on various topics. He would argue with them as if he were a lawyer, demanding that they use logic to back up their views. Marshall later recalled, "Oh yes, we talked about the law. We fussed about it and argued and carried on. I got the idea of being a lawyer from arguing with my dad....We'd argue about everything." The one thing they didn't argue about was racial segregation. "We saw eye-to-eye on that."[3] All in all, it is hardly surprising that Thurgood Marshall decided to become a lawyer.

Thoroughgood Marshall was born on July 2, 1908, in Baltimore, Maryland, to Willie and Norma Marshall. Thoroughgood had one brother, Aubrey, who was three years older than he was. When Thoroughgood was six and about to enter first grade, he began telling people to call him "Thurgood." He complained that his given name, Thoroughgood, was too complicated and too hard to spell. His mother gave Thurgood permission to change the name on his birth certificate.

Thurgood attended a small redbrick school called Number 103. Although the school was segregated, it was an excellent elementary school. When he was seven, Thurgood got an after-school job at a local grocery store. His job was to pick out items ordered by customers and then deliver them in his little red wagon. Willie and Norma insisted that their sons study hard and get good grades at school. By the time Thurgood was in the seventh grade, he got such high grades that his teachers let him skip to the eighth grade before finishing the seventh. In 1921, Thurgood began ninth grade at Baltimore's only black high school, the Colored High and Training School.

In 1924, Willie Marshall could no longer work on the railroad because of an illness. Norma worked as a substitute teacher and playground director, and Aubrey was away at college. To help his family, Thurgood worked part-time at his father's former job on the railroad.

In 1926, Thurgood joined his brother, Aubrey, at Lincoln University in Oxford, Pennsylvania. His grades were good enough for him to be admitted without an examination. In answer to a question on his application regarding his plans for his life's work, Thurgood wrote "lawyer." At Lincoln, Thurgood joined the debating team and took part in debates at various other colleges. In 1929, Thurgood married Vivian Burey, a freshman at the University of Pennsylvania.

Marshall graduated from Lincoln with honors in 1930. He then went on to attend law school at Howard University. He was prevented from going to his first choice, the University of Maryland Law School, by that institution's segregationist policies. In 1933, he graduated magna cum laude from Howard.

Now that he had a law degree, Marshall began a private law practice in Baltimore. Unfortunately, it was a very difficult time to make any money as a beginning attorney. The United States was in the midst of the Great Depression, and it was hard for Marshall to find clients who could afford a lawyer. For the NAACP in 1934, Marshall made some fact-finding trips with Charles Houston, the Dean of Howard Law School, to investigate segregation in the schools in the South. He was paid less than $5,000 a year by the NAACP.

The following year, Marshall worked on a major civil rights case, *Murray* v. *Pearson*. Donald Murray, an African-American student, sued R. A. Pearson, president of the University of Maryland, for refusing to admit him to the university's law school because of his race. Pearson stuck by the university's separate-but-equal policies. In 1936 the case was decided in favor of Murray. In winning the case, Marshall felt he had gotten revenge against the University of Maryland for previously turning him away.

Holding a poster against racial bias in Mississippi are four of the most active leaders in the NAACP movement, from left: Henry L. Moon, director of public relations; Roy Wilkins, executive secretary; Herbert Hill, labor secretary, and Thurgood Marshall.

Marshall became director of the NAACP's Legal Defense and Education Fund. His work involved him in many important cases that sought to chip away at separate but equal policies, especially regarding education. In the coming years, he would argue thirty-two cases before the U.S. Supreme Court, winning twenty-nine of them.

In 1952, as leader of a team of NAACP lawyers, Marshall began working on the famous case of *Brown* v. *Board of Education of Topeka, Kansas*. In 1896, the Supreme Court, in *Plessy* v. *Ferguson*, had ruled in favor of the principle of separate but equal, which upheld the legality of segregated facilities. Now, the Supreme Court would reach a different conclusion. On May 17, 1954, Chief Justice Earl Warren in his written opinion stated:

> *To separate [some schoolchildren] from others…solely because of their race generates a feeling of inferiority as to their status in the community that may affect their hearts and minds in a way very unlikely ever to be undone. We conclude, unanimously, that in the field of public education the doctrine of "separate but equal" has no place.*[4]

The importance of the ruling went beyond the issue of racial segregation in the public schools. It suggested that *any* form of racial segregation is unconstitutional because it is inherently unequal. The NAACP went on to argue, case by case, that if *Plessy* no longer applied to public education, it no longer applied to other facets of life.

Marshall's outstanding accomplishments eventually brought him into the government. In 1961, President John F. Kennedy nominated him to the U.S. Court of Appeals for the Second Circuit. The Senate confirmed his nomination several months later. In July 1965, President Lyndon Johnson appointed Marshall as the

Associate justice of the United States Supreme Court
Thurgood Marshall

U.S. solicitor general. Then in 1967, President Johnson nominated Marshall to the U.S. Supreme Court. Marshall became the first African-American Supreme Court justice. Throughout his years in the Supreme Court, Marshall was a strong advocate for civil rights. On cases dealing with race, Marshall believed the key was the Fourteenth Amendment, requiring equal protection and due process.

In 1991, Thurgood Marshall resigned from the Supreme Court. He died two years later, on January 24, 1993. According to former associate justice Lewis Powell, "He, in my opinion, did more to establish equal justice under the law than Martin Luther King or any other single individual. No American did more to lead our country out of the wilderness of segregation than Thurgood Marshall."[5]

Thurgood Marshall Timeline

1908—Marshall is born on July 2, in Baltimore, Maryland.

1930—Graduates with honors from Lincoln University in Pennsylvania.

1933—Graduates Howard University Law School, ranking first in his class.

1935—Argues *Murray v. Pearson* in front of the U.S. Supreme Court, and wins. The case was the first challenge of the "separate but equal" doctrine that was part of the *Plessy v. Ferguson* decision.

1936—Becomes a staff lawyer under Houston for the National Association for the Advancement of Colored People (NAACP).

1938—Becomes the lead chair in the legal office of the NAACP.

1940—Marshall is named chief of the NAACP Legal Defense and Educational Fund.

1954—Argues *Brown* v. *Board of Education of Topeka* in front of the U.S. Supreme Court, and wins.

1961—Marshall is nominated to the U.S. Court of Appeals for the Second Circuit. His confirmation is delayed for several months.

1965— President Lyndon B. Johnson names Marshall U.S. solicitor general in July.

1967—Marshall becomes an associate justice of the Supreme Court of the United States on August 30.

1991—Retires from the U.S. Supreme Court.

1993—Thurgood Marshall dies on January 24, in Bethesda, Maryland.

Civil Rights Timeline

1863—President Abraham Lincoln issues the Emancipation Proclamation on January 1, declaring that all slaves in states supporting Confederacy are now free.

1895—Booker T. Washington gives his "Atlanta Compromise" speech.

1903—W. E. B. Du Bois publishes *The Souls of Black Folk*, rejecting the "Compromise."

1909—The National Association for the Advancement of Colored People (NAACP) is formed.

1910—The National Urban League is formed.

1941—A. Philip Randolph organizes the March on Washington Movement in January.

1942—James Farmer and others form the Committee of Racial Equality (CORE) in April.

1947—CORE organizes the Journey of Reconciliation.

1948—Malcolm X joins the Nation of Islam while in prison.

1954—U.S. Supreme Court, in *Brown* v. *Board of Education of Topeka, Kansas*, rules on May 17 that separate facilities in education are unequal. Thurgood Marshall argued case for Brown.

1955—Rosa Parks is arrested in Montgomery, Alabama, for refusing to give her seat on bus to a white passenger on December 1.

1956—On December 20, the U.S Supreme Court rules that Alabama's bus segregation laws are unconstitutional.

1957—Dr. Martin Luther King, Jr., and Ralph Abernathy form the Southern Christian Leadership Conference (SCLC).

1961—Congress of Racial Equality (CORE), led by James Farmer, organizes a series of Freedom Rides to desegregate transportation facilities in South.

1963—Dr. Martin Luther King, Jr., gives his "I Have a Dream" speech to 250,000 people at Lincoln Memorial during March on Washington for Jobs and Freedom on August 28.

John Lewis elected chairman of the Student Nonviolent Coordinating Committee (SNCC).

1964—Fannie Lou Hamer, as vice chairman of Mississippi Freedom Democratic party, speaks at Democratic National Convention in Atlantic City, New Jersey.

Passage of Civil Rights Act of 1964.

1965—Malcolm X is assassinated on February 21.

Dr. King leads march from Selma to Montgomery, Alabama, in March.

Passage of Voting Rights Act of 1965.

1967—Thurgood Marshall becomes first African-American Supreme Court justice.

1968—Martin Luther King, Jr., is assassinated on April 4.

Shirley Chisholm becomes first black woman elected to Congress.

1986—John Lewis elected to Congress, representing Georgia's 5th Congressional District.

2008—Barack Obama is elected president of the United States on November 4.

Chapter Notes

Introduction

1. Adam Fairclough, *Better Day Coming: Blacks and Equality, 1890--2000* (New York: Viking, 2001), p. 39.
2. Fred Powledge, *Free At Last? The Civil Rights Movement and the People Who Made It* (Boston: Little, Brown and Company, 1991), page facing the copyright page.
3. Fairclough, p. 43.
4. Stephen B. Oates, *Let the Trumpet Sound: The Life of Martin Luther King, Jr.* (New York: Harper & Row, Publishers, 1982), p. 261.
5. Malcolm X, *The Autobiography of Malcolm X* (as told to Alex Haley) (New York: Ballantine Books, 1965), p. 401.
6. Jennifer Loven and Nancy Benac, "Packing a Nation's Hopes, Obama Rides Rails to D.C.," Associated Press, January 17, 2009.
7. President Barack Obama's Inaugural Address, January 20, 2009. Associated Press.

Chapter 1
W. E. B. Du Bois

1. David Levering Lewis, *W. E. B. Du Bois: Biography of a Race: 1868–1919* (New York: Henry Holt and Company, 1993), p. 15.
2. Ibid., p. 11.
3. Ibid., p. 33.
4. Adam Fairclough, *Better Day Coming: Blacks and Equality, 1890–2000* (New York: Viking, 2001), p. 75.
5. David Levering Lewis, *W. E. B. Du Bois: Biography of a Race: 1868–1919* (New York: Henry Holt and Company, 1993), p. 434.

Chapter 2

A. Philip Randolph

1. Jervis Anderson, *A. Philip Randolph: A Biographical Portrait* (Berkeley: University of California Press, 1972), p. 46.
2. Ibid., p. 52.
3. Ibid., p. 53.
4. Paul Boyer, *The Enduring Vision: A History of the American People* (Boston, Houghton Mifflin Company, 2002), p. 551.
5. Ibid., p. 576.
6. Anderson, opposite copyright page.

Chapter 3

Martin Luther King Jr.

1. Martin Luther King, Jr., *The Autobiography of Martin Luther King, Jr.* (New York: Warner Books, 1998), p. 7.
2. Stephen B. Oates, *Let the Trumpet Sound: The Life of Martin Luther King, Jr.* (New York: Harper & Row, Publishers, 1982), p. 9.
3. Ibid.
4. King, p. 14.
5. Ibid., p. 60.
6. Martin Luther King, Jr., *A Testament of Hope: The Essential Writings of Martin Luther King, Jr.* (San Francisco: Harper & Row, Publishers, 1986), p. 301.
7. Ibid., p. 219.
8. Ibid., p. 286.

Chapter 4
James Farmer

1. James Farmer, *Lay Bare the Heart: An Autobiography of the Civil Rights Movement* (New York: Arbor House, 1985), p. 31.
2. Ibid., p. 58.
3. Ibid., p. 74.
4. Ibid., p. 69.
5. Ibid., p. 351.

Chapter 5
Malcolm X

1. Malcolm X, *The Autobiography of Malcolm X* (as told to Alex Haley) (New York: Ballantine Books, 1965), pp. 41–42.
2. Ibid., p. 49.
3. Ibid., p. 86.
4. Ibid., p. 173.
5. Ibid., pp. 216–217.
6. Adam Fairclough, *Better Day Coming: Blacks and Equality, 1890-2000* (New York: Viking, 2001), p. 310.
7. Malcolm X, p. 416.
8. Ibid., p. xvi.

Chapter 6
John Lewis

1. John Lewis, *Walking with the Wind* (San Diego: Harcourt Brace & Company, 1998), p. 30.
2. Ibid., p. 31.
3. Fred Powledge, *Free At Last? The Civil Rights Movement and the People Who Made It* (Boston: Little, Brown and Company, 1991), p. 110.

4. Lewis, p. 65.
5. Ibid., p. 220.
6. Ibid., p. 489.

Chapter 7
Fannie Lou Hamer

1. Kay Mills, *This Little Light of Mine: The Life of Fannie Lou Hamer* (New York: Dutton, 1993), pp. 7–8.
2. Ibid., p. 9.
3. Ibid., p. 13.
4. Peter John Ling, *Gender and the Civil Rights Movement* (New York: Garland Pubishers, 1999), p. 153.
5. Lynne Olson, *Freedom's Daughters: The Unsung Heroines of the Civil Rights Movement from 1830 to 1970* (New York: Scribner, 2001), p. 319.
6. Mills, p. 18.

Chapter 8
Thurgood Marshall

1. Juan Williams, *Thurgood Marshall: American Revolutionary* (New York: Random House, 1998), p. 35.
2. Ibid.
3. Ibid., pp. 35–36.
4. Karen O'Connor and Larry J. Sabato, *American Government: Continuity and Change* (New York: Longman, 2002), p. 190.
5. Williams, p. 400.

Glossary

American Civil War—The war between the northern and southern states of the United States that occurred between 1861 and 1865.

assassination—The murder of an important or famous person.

civil rights—The rights of every citizen of a country. In the United States, a citizen's civil rights include the right to vote, the right to live anywhere, and the right to equal protection under the law.

Congress of Racial Equality (CORE)—A United States civil rights organization that originally played a pivotal role for African Americans in the civil rights movement.

Emancipation Proclamation—Executive order by President Abraham Lincoln that freed the slaves in the Confederate States of America; the formal proclamation was made on January 1, 1863.

Jim Crow laws—Laws enacted primarily in the South from the 1880s through 1910 that enforced racial separation. Jim Crow was the name of a character in a minstrel show. Its characters were white performers who blackened their faces and made fun of African Americans.

Ku Klux Klan (KKK)—A race-hate group started after the Civil War.

lynching—Ilegal killing, usually by hanging; a murder committed by a mob of people.

National Association for the Advancement of Colored People (NAACP)—An organization started to help all Americans gain equal rights and protection under the law. The NAACP is one of the oldest civil rights organizations in the United States.

racism—A belief that race is the primary factor determining human traits and capacities, and that racial differences produce an inherent superiority of a particular race.

sharecropper—A tenant farmer who is provided with credit for seed, tools, living quarters, and food; who works the land; and who receives an agreed-upon share of the value of the crop minus charges.

slavery—The buying and selling of human beings.

Socialism—A system in which the means of production and distribution of goods are owned and controlled by government or the community as a whole.

Southern Christian Leadership Conference (SCLC)—An African-American civil rights organization founded in 1957 and closely associated with its first president, Dr. Martin Luther King, Jr.

Vietnam War—A protracted military conflict (1954-1975) between the Communist forces of North Vietnam supported by China and the Soviet Union and the non-Communist forces of South Vietnam supported by the United States.

World War I—A war fought between 1914 and 1918 mainly in Europe. Great Britain, France, Russia, Italy, the United States, and their allies fought against Germany and its allies.

World War II—A war fought between 1939 and 1945 mainly in Europe, northern Africa, and Asia and the Atlantic and Pacific oceans. Great Britain, France, the Soviet Union, the United States, China, and their allies fought against Germany, Italy, Japan, and their allies.

Alder, David A. *Heroes For Civil Rights*. New York: Holiday House, 2008.

Bausum, Ann. *Freedom Riders: John Lewis and Jim Zwerg on the Front Lines of the Civil Rights Movement*. Washington, D.C.: National Geographic, 2006.

Crowe, Chris. *Thurgood Marshall: A Twentieth-Century Life*. New York: Viking, 2008.

Draper, Allison Stark. *The Assassination of Malcolm X*. New York: Rosen Pub. Group, 2002.

Miller, Calvin Craig. *A. Philip Randolph and the African American Labor Movement*. Greensboro, N.C.: Morgan Reynolds Pub., 2005.

Stafford, Mark. *W. E. B. Du Bois: Scholar and Activist*. Philadelphia: Chelsea House, 2005.

Internet Addresses

African American World

<http://www.pbs.org/wnet/aaworld/timeline/civil_01.html>

Black Leaders of the Civil Rights Movement

<http://www.georgiaencyclopedia.org/nge/Feature.jsp?id=s-51>

National Civil Rights Museum

<http://www.civilrightsmuseum.org/?page_id=434>

We Shall Overcome: Historic Places of the Civil Rights Movement

<http://www.nps.gov/nr/travel/civilrights/change.htm>